BOXER'S SHORTS

More than just a Brief attempt at Humor

4

THE MUSIC BOOK

For Everyone in the Magical World of Music;
Performers, Conductors, Their Admirers and Patrons,
and for Anyone Looking for a Healthy Laugh or Chuckle

With Best Wishes
Rohenton Bryan

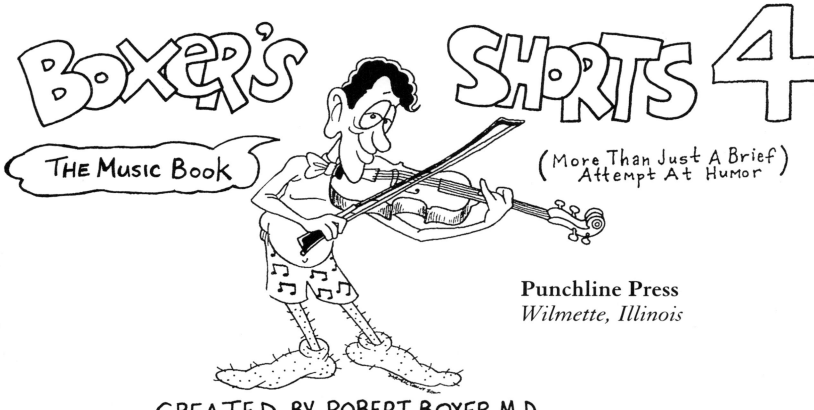

Boxer's Shorts 4

The Music Book

(More Than Just A Brief) Attempt At Humor

Punchline Press
Wilmette, Illinois

CREATED BY ROBERT BOXER M.D.
ILLUSTRATED BY DARNELL TOWNS

Book and Cover Design
Darnell Towns/Robert Boxer

Typesetting and Production Services
Sans Serif, Inc.

Cover Illustration
Darnell Towns

Back Cover Photograph
Self-Timer)

Published by Punchline Press
P.O. Box 308, Wilmette, Illinois 60091

Printed in the United States of America

First Edition, May, 2006

Library of Congress Catalog Number 2005910610
ISBN 13: 978-0-9620687-3-7
ISBN 10: 0-9620687-3-X

Contents

Dedication

To my wife, Marsha (Cissy), for sharing her lifelong appreciation and interest in music, especially classical, and allowing her enthusiasm to rub off on me.

To the memory of my late in-laws, Dr. Jacob and Mrs. Rose Levin of Cincinnati, who were so important and involved in bringing good music to Cincinnati, and providing an environment for their children to appreciate and enjoy this wonderful gift.

To the memory of the late Richard Tucker, the great American tenor, who through my wife and her family became a valued acquaintance who shared many musical and other happy moments with us.

To the memory of the late Ray Nordstrand, who had a 52 year association with WFMT-FM as General Manager, President, Host and Consultant. His unceasing efforts and direction made WFMT-FM one of the most respected fine arts stations in the world.

Illustrator's Dedication

I thank God each and every day for bestowing upon me such a rare gift and for putting family in my life who have been so supportive.

Foreword

At the same time that he practices innovative medicine in the field of allergy, Dr. Robert W. Boxer is one very punny guy! Bob thinks and breathes in the language of pun. It is a fitting tribute to his unique and wonderful mind that Bob was named "Punster of the Year" by the International Save the Pun Foundation. Bob, his wife Marsha, and their children have been like family to me for almost all of the 29 years I have been performing with the Chicago Symphony Orchestra.

Sometimes Bob's puns are hilariously funny, sometimes a bit obscure. However, the obscure ones often become hilariously funny after digesting them for a while. We are also especially fortunate that Darnell Towns, Bob's talented illustrator for his three previous books, has once again brought to visual life the fruits of Bob's fertile imagination.

In this fourth book of the Boxer's Shorts series, Bob delves into the varied and beautiful world of Music. Bob and Marsha are a couple of the most devoted and passionate music lovers that I know. They have attended countless performances and rehearsals of symphony, opera, chamber music and solo recitals. The radio is almost always playing music in the Boxer home. I know that as they are attentively absorbing the music, Bob's imagination is racing to create new puns and re-call old favorites. He reaches for those pun ingredients, seasons them, cooks them up, and then serves them to us for our enjoyment.

There is definitely something in *BOXER'S SHORTS 4* for everyone. If you are a musician or a music-lover, the puns on the following pages will no doubt strike

many familiar resonating chords. For those readers who are not musicians, this collection of wit and wisdom may hopefully pique your interest to listen to a string quartet, or a symphony with a prominent part for the E-flat Clarinet or Tuba!

Enjoy!

John Bruce Yeh
Assistant Principal and Solo E-flat Clarinet
Chicago Symphony Orchestra

Preface

This fourth book of pun cartoons conceived by myself and illustrated again by Darnell Towns is devoted to pun cartoons that have to do with Music, mostly classical, including opera. This book should particularly be appealing to musicians of all ages, at all levels of talent, and to all those who enjoy musical performances, as well as to anyone who enjoys this type of illustrated humor.

Those who have read our earlier three books are aware that my penchant is visualization of situations lending themselves to illustration as pun cartoons, and Darnell Towns has the unique ability to translate this humor into a very enjoyable art form.

Almost all of the work created in this book, and the other books, is original in the sense that, with few exceptions, I have not seen nor heard the humor previously spoken, written, or drawn in a similar context. I suspect that no one can be aware of all that has preceded, and surely similar ideas must arise simultaneously. Therefore original in this sense means not knowingly incited or stimulated by the works or thoughts of others.

This book also incorporates several cartoons from the first three books in the series, and also incorporates two cartoons that were suggested by a friend, Susan Cherry, a very talented published poet, and these cartoons appear on pages 14 and 98.

The pun on the front cover is one that I heard as a teenager. The cartoon on page 135 was created by Darnell Towns and myself.

I'm appreciative of the efforts of Stephanie Bockhol of A-OK Business Service in Skokie, IL for painstakingly typing and retyping the text and corrections and revisions. As with our previous works, I hope that our readers enjoy the blending of original humor and art that we have put together in this collection.

"NATURALLY WE ARE STARTING WITH SCALES."

A STRING QUARTET

"I'm upset. Those men are making Overtures."

PIRACY ON THE HIGH SEAS.

"LOIS HAS ALWAYS WANTED TO BE AN OPRAH SINGER."

"I HEARD YOU WERE LOOKING FOR SOMEONE WITH A HIGHER REGISTER."

9

"THIS IS MR. VERDI. I'M HIRING HIM TO HELP FIGURE OUT WHO ARE THE REAL STAFF AND WHO ARE THE FALSTAFF.

11

"HE'S ALSO THE FIRST STRING QUARTERBACK."

13

"AIRPORT SECURITY IS CONFISCATING MORE AND MORE "BAND" OBJECTS."

14

AARON COPLAND COMPOSING.

16

"GET A LOAD OF THAT CARRY-OKE."

"REMEMBER, WHEN DR. SMITH DOES OPEN HEART SURGERY HE ONLY LIKES TO LISTEN TO CHAMBER MUSIC."

"Now I Know why they call this Restaurant "Trios.""

19

"IS THIS HANDEL'S WATER MUSIC."

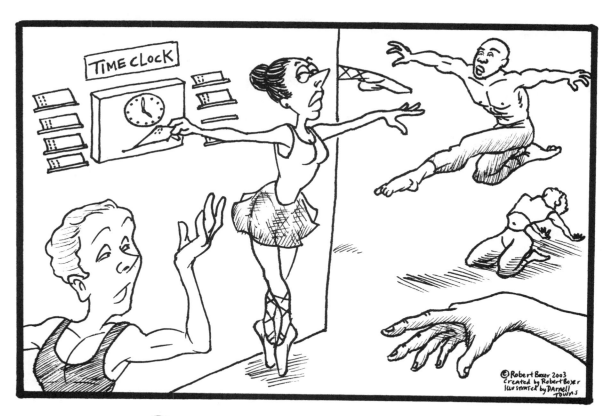

DANCE OF THE HOURS.

"Now I have the inspiration for the **TITAN** Symphony."

"WOULD YOU GET A LOAD OF THAT HORN SECTION."

"I THINK BETWEEN THE TWO JUKEBOXES, HE'S GOING TO MAUL HER."

27

WHEN SECURITY APPREHENDED HIM HE WAS TAKEN A BACH.

"THERE MUST BE SOME MISUNDERSTANDING. I ASKED THE MUSICAL DIRECTOR TO BE SURE THAT THE *SHEET* MUSIC WAS IN MY HOTEL ROOM."

29

JOHN BRUCE YEH PLAYING THE CLARINET IN E-FLAT.

TCHAIKOVSKY'S "DANCE OF THE TUMBLERS"

TRULY AN INSTRUMENTAL PIECE.

THE BACH DOUBLE CONCERTO

"MY PHYSICIAN SAID I WAS DEPRESSED AND I SHOULD EITHER TAKE MEDICATION OR GET A **HANDEL.**"

35

"QUICK, WE'RE BEING ROBBED AND THEY'RE GETTING AWAY WITH THE **LUTE**!"

37

"I REALIZE YOU'RE A FAMOUS SINGER, IS THAT WHY YOU'RE ASKING TO SERVE YOUR SENTENCE IN SINGSING?"

39

PROKOFIEV'S "THE LOVE OF 3 ORANGES."

"THIS IS GREAT! I ALWAYS THOUGHT THE MIKADO WAS A SWISS WATCH!"

45

TRULY THE FIRST VIOLINIST.

"As your voice teacher, let me be the first to say 'It's about time you found it.'"

"I GUESS YOU KNOW THE "KEY" HE WILL PLAY IN."

SIR EDWARD ELGAR'S "THE EMPIRE MARCH"

"THAT'S OUR HEAD CHEF. BEFORE HE PREPARES A MEAL HE LIKES TO PLAY VIVALDI'S "FOUR SEASONS.""

VIVALDI'S `THE FOUR SEASONS.'

49

"THESE INSPIRE ME TO COMPOSE ORCHESTRAL SUITES."

53

"I GUESS HER MOTHER'S HARPING FINALLY PAID OFF."

A CADEMY OF ST. MARTIN IN THE FIELDS

"GUESS WHICH **BALLET** I'M WRITING?"

59

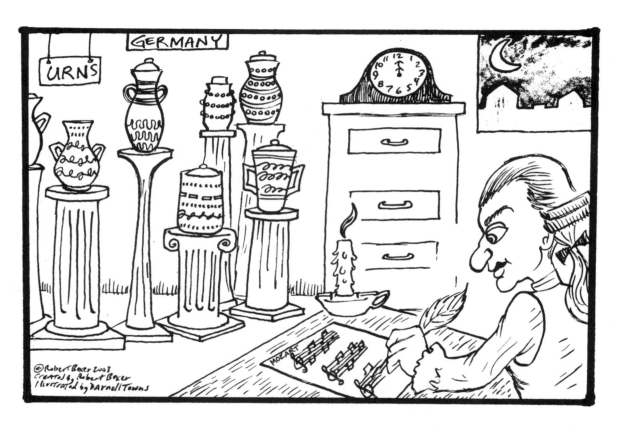

"THIS IS MY INSPIRATION FOR A NACHT-URN."

60

TWO PICKPOCKETS WORKING IN CONCERT.

63

A PIECE FOR TUBAS

TERESA REILLY REACHING REALLY HIGH NOTES WITH HER CLARINET.

"I'M SURE I'M GOING TO GET MY BASS SOON."

"You can skip the beverage, I just stopped in for some BARTALK."

"I MAY NOT HAVE MUCH, BUT AT LEAST I CAN
AFFORD THIS."

Eine kleine Nachtmusik (A LITTLE NIGHT MUSIC)

72

THROWN OUT STEALING 2ND BASS.

"She had perfect pitch and I want you to do the same."

"Oops! I guess this isn't exactly the type of BASS Camp that we intended to bring Seymour to."

"Maybe you're allergic to Cello mold."

"OH GOSH, I THOUGHT THIS WAS ABOUT A MUSIC COMPOSER."

ROCK CONCERT

THE LYRICIST

BEETHOVEN'S CORAL FANTASY

"NOW, THIS LADY IS A FAMOUS SINGER, SO MAKE SURE THE ROOF HAS PERFECT PITCH."

"I'M LOOKING FOR AN EXTENSION CHORD JUST IN CASE
I'M ASKED TO PLAY AN ENCORE."

85

"YOU SHOULD REALLY BE SINGING IN A HIGHER REGISTER."

HANDEL'S INSPIRATION FOR "MUSIC FOR THE ROYAL FIREWORKS."

FROM SEA TO SHINING SEA.

"No, I said 'Bring Your Double BASS.'"

91

"You better not try to fiddle with that."

"Wow, Just Look at that Kathleen BATTLE!"

"HE MUST'VE THOUGHT HE WOULD TURN INTO A MARVELOUS VIOLINIST."

97

"NOW I FEEL COMFORTABLE
ENOUGH WITH BOEING THAT
I CAN CONFIDENTLY AUDITION."

99

"No, No. This Piece calls For Four Hands."

101

SCHUBERT'S TROUT QUINTET.

"I'M SORRY, I DIDN'T MEAN TO INTERFERE WITH THE CONCERT. I SAID, "MY STROH'S.""

"O BOE, PLEASE DON'T LET ME DOWN."

"THIS PART OF 'SIEGFRIED' IS CALLED 'THE FOREST MURMURS' AND HAS NOTHING TO DO WITH THE HUMAN HEART SO PUT YOUR STETHOSCOPE AWAY."

TALES FROM THE VIENNA WOODS

108

"OH, THAT'S SCHUBERT'S NINTH, NO WONDER THEY CALL IT THE GRATE SYMPHONY."

"THIS MUST BE THE ROBERT SHAW CHORALE."

"DARNELL, IF WE'RE GOING TO STAY IN THE CAR YOU'RE GOING TO HAVE TO COME UP WITH A CAR-TUNE."

SERENADE FOR STRINGS BY ANTONIN DVORAK.

"I THOUGHT WE WERE PLAYING IN THE METRONOME."

HE'S A TRUE LYRICIST.

115

"WELL, YOU DID ASK ME TO DESIGN A LOW KEY STUDIO FOR YOU."

"THERE'S NO MORE ROOM ON THE BOARD SO I'LL KEEP YOUR KEYS IN MY POCKET. THE OWNER INSISTS I STOP AT 88."

119

"I GUESS THEY WERE INSTRUMENTAL IN WINNING THE WAR."

AFTER A RECORD 35 ENCORES AT RAVINIA,
DAWN FINALLY BREAKS.

"THIS MUST BE THE **BOSTON POPS**."

TEMPEST IN A TEAPOT

125

THE WIND ENSEMBLE

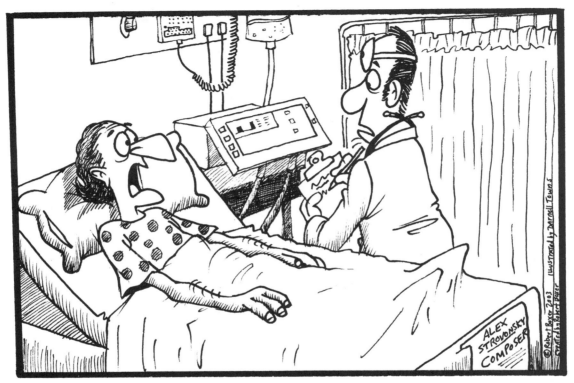

PATIENT: "DOCTOR, I'M HAVING TROUBLE WITH CONSTIPATION."
DOCTOR: "YOU KNOW, THE FIRST MOVEMENT IS ALWAYS THE MOST DIFFICULT."

127

"THIS IS MY **SHOW PAN**."

130

"WOULD YOU LIKE TO SEE MY BUTTERFLY COLLECTION."

132

133

"YES, ALL OF **SIBELIUS'** SYMPHONIES WERE FINNISH(ED)."

135

"Bob, I sure hope your **pun tunes** keep us afloat".

Acknowledgments
(The Guilty Parties)

For encouragement and support of the creative (?) process that led to this collection of pun cartoons, I'm especially indebted to: very good friends Bill, Zehava, Eitan and Naomi Frankel. Bill painstakingly reviewed all of the cartoons, as he has done for the previous books. Bill and Zehava are not only good friends, but Bill is also an excellent copyright attorney, and his advice, and Zahava's support has again been invaluable; good friends Nancy Janus and Marcia Steinberg, both of whom typed descriptions of many of the cartoons and made comments and helpful suggestions.

Others who have been particularly encouraging and helpful include George Pepper, a retired physician, and an extremely knowledgeable connoisseur of opera, often appearing as a supernumerary at The Lyric Opera of Chicago, for his help in some of the specific areas of music; Linda Forman, a good friend and popular area CPA, for her ongoing support of my mischievous penchant for punning; and Drs. Leonard Berlin, Joshua Epstein, Michael Lewis, Alexander Golbin, Arkady Rapoport, Julia Litvin, Naphtali Gutstein (an Ophthalmologist, who could easily write many books on humor, especially pun), Coleman Seskind, a long time, very good friend, Alon Winnie, Tom Stone, Allan Lieberman, William Rea, Ken Gerdes, Mort Teich, David Buscher, Charlie Hinshaw, Frank Waickman, Rich Hrdlicka, Wayne Konetzki, Timothy Hain, Bill Kerr, Jim Holland, Tom Keeler, Keith Sarpolis, Emily Gottlieb, Shirley Forbes, John McMahon, Mick Meiselman, Bill Myers, Charles Wolfe, Jacqueline Willrich, Bill Fagman, Larry Elegant, Joseph Leija, Charlie Swarts (one of my instructors in allergy and a punster with the quickest wit that I have ever known), Len Drucker, Doris Rapp,

Jerry Bernstein, Doug Cook, Joel Sanders, Herbert Lippitz, Harold Shafter, Dave Fretzin, Robert LaPata, Tony Daddono, Hugh Falls, Leigh Rosenblum, Phil Krause, Martin Kaplan, Robert Stanley, William Kehoe, Robert Bastian, Steven Devries, Gary Morris, Salmon Goldberg, David Chudwin, Noga Askenazi, Bernard Hankin, David Lee, Mort Doblin, Sun-Bum Kim, Renee Reich, Wayne Wirtz, Sushil Sharma, Pat Ebenhoeh, Joe LaMothe, Bruce Berkson, Steven Meyers, Herb Greenfield, George Burica, Dolly Thomas, and Sue Rossman.

Musicians who have been especially supportive include Claudia Kerski-Nienow and her husband Mark Nienow, who have been important members of the Chicago Lyric Opera Chorus for many years, and who have often appeared with their daughter Nicole in productions; Jeri Lou Zike, an excellent violinist who appears with the Ravinia Festival Orchestra and other prominent venues, and Nancy Mazurowski, a very good singer and music teacher.

Others who have been especially supportive include the following: Mary Jo and David Reilly, Mary and Gordon Yeh, Jenna Yeh, Kerry and John Faro, Ord Matek, A.S.C.W., an author and neighbor, Shelly and Elliot Abramson (long time friends and supporters from early-on), Verne Bengtson, Michael and Frada Boxer, Eric Boxer, Russell Boxer (my godson and very clever heir-apparent punster), Jack Boxer from Detroit, Phil, Florine, Susan and Sarah Boxer, Martin and Helen Boxer, Judy and Jack Wartell, Lisa and Ed Stein (Lisa is a very creative TV producer, writer, and editor, and her husband Ed is a successful and popular political cartoonist for the Rocky Mountain

News), Gregory Opelka, Carol Hopwood, Chuck and Miriam Cohn, Rebecca Crown, Eric Robb, Erica Cherry, Lois Gartenberg, Joan and Don Shrensky, Donna and Herschel Levine, Bud and Georgia Photopulous, Jim Frankenbach, Peter Butler, Stacy Sochacki, Tony DiLorenzo, Lyle Kay, Judith Goldberg, Sue Jahnke, Donna Bouroudjian, Linda Balogh, Jeanne Esposito, Tracy Anderson, Connie Tschudy, Ann Hankin, Sharon Kane, Valerie Kramer, Becky Leija, Sheila and Howard Pizer, Kay Samec, Avery Delotte, David Hochman, Karyn and Jeff Feinsilver, Marcy and Alan Gilbert, Marci Good, Marjorie Fisher, Andrew Fisher, Diane Kubis, Howard, Nancy, Stephanie, Christopher and Nick Bultinck, Nick Mechales, Scott Friedrich (one of the youngest and cleverist riddle makers that I have ever met), Dick Boylan, Joe Bobak, Joe Bobak, Jr., Danny Bobak, Tom Krettler, Dan Hales, John Eisenbart, John and Mitzi Bogacki, Tony Maita, Jim Van Overbake, Bob Herguth, Chris Moriarty-Field and Mark Field, George Carpenter, Barbara Kravets, Bonnie Minsky, Elisa Yochim, David Tuttle (a talented clarinetist and very clever punster), Karen Eness, Lynn and Courtney Lawson, Jack and Devorah Isaacs, Scott Lewis, and his wife Camille Witos (she is a terrific pianist and was my piano teacher for two years), Mary Schuette, Sondra Kraff, Rachel and Hillel Lifson, David and Miriam Forman, Jack and Fran Mabley, June Winnie, Mary Ellen Dalicandro, Marie Burns, Louise and Bob White, and Sarah and Chuck Orlove (they have sat directly behind my wife and myself at the Lyric Opera for the past 20 years, and by their knowledge and interest and their personable company, have enhanced our appreciation and enjoyment immensely).

139

Especially supportive have been Dr. Gary Oberg, and his nurse Jan Beima, who by laughing at my puns at many medical meetings, have intentionally or inadvertently encouraged me to continue.

Besides being indebted to my wife Marsha, and my sons Stephen and Richard, who have been helpful in so many ways, I am also appreciative of my wonderful daughter-in-law Lisa (Stephen's wife), and her mother, Barbara Soibel, her brother Randy Soibel, her late father, Larry Soibel, her aunt Joyce Dry, Mark, Sally, Mason, Jake, Austin, Gweneth, and Brent Schiller, Amy, Sandy, and Lissy Rabin, Suzanne and Ken Lyon, and Bobbi and Dr. Richard Litt, of Coral Gables, FL, who have been so active and supportive in bringing good music to South Florida.

My seven year old grandson, Jake Morgan Boxer, is beginning to understand puns and he is very bright, precious, cute, enthusiastic, entertaining and amusing, and helps to keep me in a humorous and loving mood.

Since the last book, we have also been blessed with twin grandchildren, Jordaan Mayer Boxer and Nicole Kendall Boxer, who are now five years old.

Nicole particularly enjoys dancing, while Jordaan seems to take to musical instruments, and their big brother, Jake, sings very well. It will be exciting for Marsha and me to see what all three grandchildren do with their interests in the future.

I am indebted to Bonnie Pick, also a Northwestern graduate and supporter, a musicology major, who has been a companion especially to my wife, but often to both of us, in attending musical events at the Ravinia Festival, as well as the Steans Institute for Young Artists, the Ravinia chamber music concerts, and many excellent musical events at Northwestern University.

It has been my wife's and my great pleasure over the past 25 years to have John Bruce Yeh, Assistant Principal Clarinetist of the Chicago Symphony Orchestra, and Founder and Director of the Grammy winning Chicago Pro Musica, as a good friend and supporter of my endeavors in punning, as well as our family's interest in music. John also has helped in preparation of this book by reviewing the cartoons and text. John's wife, Teresa Reilly, also a gifted clarinetist, is a good friend and also very supportive of my weakness for punning.

I have also had the great pleasure of knowing, through my wife and her family, three outstanding stars of The Metropolitan Opera, and their families: the late great American tenor, Richard Tucker; the brilliant, versatile, internationally renown American Soprano, Roberta Peters; and, especially during the 20 years that he was Musical Director of The Ravinia Festival, Maestro James Levine, Conductor, Musical and Artistic Director of The Metropolitan Opera, and now also the Boston Symphony.

Getting to know these outstanding musical talents on a personal level was very gratifying, as they were and are generous, sincere, considerate, and all them possessed an incredibly enjoyable sense of humor.

To all of these very dear people, and to all those inadvertently omitted, I'm deeply appreciative of your support and encouragement, but please remember that many of you are guilty of aiding and abetting a punster.

About the Author

Dr. Robert W. Boxer is a practicing Allergist with an office in the Professional Building of the Old Orchard Center in Skokie, Illinois a suburb of Chicago. Bob has created thousands of pun cartoons, almost all of them have been illustrated by Darnell Towns. For four years, pun cartoons incorporating the themes of Medicine and Sports appeared regularly in *THE MAIN EVENT, a Monthly Sports Journal for Physicians.*

Bob's first book, *BOXER SHORTS, More Than Just a Brief Attempt at Humor,* illustrated by Darnell Towns, was published in 1988. The second book *BOXER SHORTS, Round 2, More Than Just a Brief Attempt at Humor,* also illustrated by Darnell Towns was published in 1994. The third book *BOXER SHORTS 3, The Medical Version, More Than Just a Brief Attempt at Humor,* also illustrated by Darnell Towns, was published in 2001.

After graduating from Southwest High School in Kansas City, Missouri, Bob earned his pre-medical degree at the University of Denver, where, among other elective courses, he took music appreciation. Bob then moved to Chicago to attend Northwestern University Medical School and he served his internship and residency at Cook County Hospital in Chicago and trained in Allergy at the University of Illinois College of Medicine where he taught for a number of years. Chicago provided a unique opportunity to enjoy all kinds of music, including The Lyric Opera of Chicago, The Ravinia Festival, Grant Park, and the world renown Chicago Symphony Orchestra. Currently Bob is on the active medical staff at Rush North Shore Medical Center in Skokie, Illinois, and on the emeritus attending staff at Lutheran General Hospital in Park Ridge, Illinois.

He is a fellow of a number of professional medical and allergy societies.

Bob was named Punster of the Year by the International Save the Pun Foundation in 1993.

Bob and Marsha have been season subscribers to the Lyric Opera of Chicago for 34 years, and they were for a time season subscribers to the Chicago Symphony Orchestra Concerts. Marsha still attends many concerts at the CSO and Bob does occasionally. Both are very frequent attendees at the Ravinia Music Festival during the summer in Highland Park, nearby Chicago, and occasionally at Grant Park in Chicago. Through their long time friendship with John Bruce Yeh, Assistant Principal Clarinetist at the CSO, they have also attended many other musical events, and have particularly enjoyed watching Molly Yeh, John's younger daughter, become an award winning (Fischoff Gold Medal) percussionist as a young teenager. Bob and Marsha attend many of the outstanding musical events at Northwestern University which has consistently been one of the perks of living in the Chicago area. They also enjoy the MYA (Midwest Young Artists), directed by talented Allan Dennis, a fantastic opportunity for young people to pursue musical interests.

Bob's wife, Marsha, frequently attends concerts at Ravinia's Martin Theatre and also the Steans Institute for Young Artists, including the Chamber Music concert series.

Since Bob obviously enjoys music and punning, and has been published as a punster, it was only natural to put together a book of pun cartoons regarding music, which to some extent emphasizes classical music and opera, although not entirely. This work has been especially inspired by the Lyric Opera of Chicago, the Ravinia Music Festival, the Chicago Symphony Orchestra, Northwestern University's excellent School of Music, and WFMT, the classical FM Radio Station.

About the Illustrator

Darnell Towns is an artist of many talents. It all began in Chicago, Illinois as a child all of three years old. After excelling in all of his art classes, Darnell finally received his Bachelor of Fine Arts in filmmaking and animation from the School of the Art Institute of Chicago. As he began his quest of becoming a full fledged professional artist, he also played drums for his church and sang in the church choir, activities which he still occasionally pursues. At the beginning of his quest, he met Dr. Robert W. Boxer, an allergist in Skokie, Illinois, who presented the wacky idea of a doctor/cartoonist collaboration. After 20 years of freelance projects, film projects, advertising campaigns, children's radio programs, comic books, comic strips, and professional pursuits in fine arts establishments, Darnell Towns is still a part of Robert W. Boxer's wacky idea of a doctor/cartoonist collaboration.

List of Cartoons

1. Scales
2. Barely Owes
3. String Quartet
4. Making Overtures
5. Piracy on High Seas
6. Oprah Singer
7. Up and Down Career
8. A Higher Register
9. Gone Offenbach
10. Who Are Falstaff
11. Keyboard at Club 88
12. First String Quarterback
13. Pictures at Exhibition
14. Confiscating Band Objects
15. Copeland Composing
16. CSO DVD Present
17. Carry-Oke
18. Chamber Music
19. Restaurant "Trios"
20. Ax To Grind
21. Giggly
22. Water Music
23. Dance of the Hours
24. Titan Symphony
25. Horn Section
26. Maul Her
27. Both Rocky 2's
28. Taken A Bach
29. Sheet Music in Room
30. Clarinet in E-flat
31. Dance of the Tumblers
32. Instrumental Piece
33. Double Concerto
34. Unravelled
35. Get A Handel
36. The Lute
37. Blue Grass
38. Kiss to Build a Dream
39. Sentence in Sing-Sing
40. Love of 3 Oranges
41. The Mikado
42. Truly First Violinist
43. Time You Found It
44. You Know The Key
45. To Key West
46. Bach is Baroque
47. The Empire March
48. Four Seasons
49. Four Seasons
50. Woodwind
51. Counter Tenor
52. Orchestral Suites
53. Jim's Drum Set
54. Organ Donor
55. Mother's Harping
56. St. Martin
57. Moscow Nut Factory
58. Beatles
59. Low and Grin
60. Nacht-Urn

61. Working in Concert
62. The Real Price
63. A Manual Ax
64. Piece For Tubas
65. Audition for Supers
66. Reaching High Notes
67. My Bass Soon
68. Some Bar Talk
69. Afford This
70. Bore A Dean
71. Nachtmusik
72. Toot Own Horn
73. Stealing 2nd Bass
74. Perfect Pitch
75. Bass Camp
76. By Jupiter
77. Cello Mold
78. Book of Lists
79. Rock Concert
80. Shrink Wrapper
81. Lyricist
82. Coral Fantasy
83. Roof Pitch
84. Trombone
85. Extension Chord
86. Singing Higher
87. Royal Fireworks
88. Rhythm
89. Firebird
90. Shining Sea

91. Double Bass
92. Compose Yourself
93. Better Not Fiddle
94. Tour And Dough
95. Kathleen Battle
96. Beethoven's Fifth
97. Shaham
98. Boeing
99. Minute Waltz
100. Four Hands
101. Maria Callous
102. WFM Tea
103. Trout Quintet
104. My Stroh's
105. Oboe
106. Forest Murmurs
107. Vienna Woods
108. Paganini's Theme
109. Grate Symphony
110. Shaw Chorale
111. Car-Tune
112. Fig, A Row
113. Serenade For Strings
114. Metronome
115. True Lyricist
116. Low Key Studio
117. Stop At 88
118. Good Enough
119. 25th Symphony
120. Winning the War